For Fiona

Best Wishes

92 96

GOLD TEAMWORK

Building and Maintaining
Your Winning Team

Bill Nelson

INFORMATION
AUSTRALIA

Published by
Information Australia
A.C.N. 006 042 173
A.B.N. 41 360 725 517
75 Flinders Lane
Melbourne Vic. 3000
Telephone: (03) 9654 2800
Fax: (03) 9650 5261
Internet: www.infoaust.com
Email: mail@infoaust.com

The National Library of Australia
Cataloguing-in-Publication entry:

Nelson, Bill.
 Gold teamwork : building and maintaining your winning team.

 ISBN 1 86350 333 1

 1. Teamwork. I. Title.

658.4036

Cover & Page Design: Ben Graham

Printed in Australia by Australian Print Group

Dedication

To my late father, Ern Nelson. No greater teacher has there been. There isn't a day that goes by where something he said doesn't get put to good use. To my mother Barbara Nelson for all the help, guidance and love over the years.

To my wife Joanne, and our children Jae, Elle and Kye. Thank you for allowing me to pursue the opportunities that this book is based upon.

To all the athletes, coaches and staff that created those opportunities.

Contents

Introduction

Teamwork - what's in a name anyway?

In just about every facet of our lives we are involved in some form of team structure. It could be in our family environment, or associated with our occupation. We could also find team structure within our sporting pursuits, regardless of whether we are a professional, an avid fan, or just in pursuit of the enjoyment and success that sport can bring.

In all these instances we are faced with opportunities to understand and to function with another individual or group. These opportunities arise through interactions, communications, relationships, and the ability to cooperate. This is the basis for successful teamwork. There are many models that have been developed to outline the theoretical structures of teamwork. As is the case in many other areas of modern-day life, we have taken something relatively simple and tried to explain it by making it more difficult than it actually is.

On October 17, 1988, I started work at the Australian Institute of Sport as an assistant swimming coach to Bill Sweetenham. During one of our many discussions on what is needed to be a better coach, Bill told me: "Many coaches see, but very few observe what is going on." This book is based on my observations of the people and the teams I have been associated with. It includes observations of my own family, to my personal sporting career, the time I spent as an apprentice coal miner in the Hunter Valley and, of course, the experiences I have had as a professional sporting coach.

The content of this book is practical rather than scientific. The principles that I will outline have been used in many different circumstances and with a variety of teams and individuals to produce successful results.

There are many different areas which can influence the success of a team, but the key components are always the people within that team. They, without a doubt, can and will provide its future. I believe the strength of a team is the team itself. If the leaders and team members can openly communicate, leave behind self-interests and egos, and work together towards a common goal, then success is almost assured. Without these developments, success will be hard, if not almost impossible to attain.

If we, as individuals, understand the basics of teamwork, then we can successfully work within a team structure. As mentioned, many things we do daily involve the format, outline or process of some type of team. Because teamwork is such a vital part of our everyday existence, it is important to make sure we are happy within that environment. At the end of the day, we are better at what we do, if we are enjoying the experience.

I hope this book creates discussion and thought. If it provides an opportunity for you to question how your team can operate more successfully, then I have achieved my goal. I hope you have the opportunity to enjoy your pursuit of creating a successful team, just as I have enjoyed the experiences that make up the content of this book.

Teamwork

The six most important words are: *I admit that I am wrong.*

The five most important words are: *You did a great job.*

The four most important words are: *What do you think.*

The three most important words are: *Could you please.*

The two most important words are: *Thank you.*

The most important word is: *We.*

The least important word is: *I.*

Inspiring Words - Peter Issacson.

Chapter 1

Roles and Responsibilities

"We are what we repeatedly do. Excellence is
therefore not an act but a habit."
Anonymous

"All my life I feared tomorrow until I decided
to live today in courage. There is nothing I can
do about yesterday. Tomorrow never comes.
I'm responsible only for today."
Inspiring Words – Peter Isaacson

Whose job is it anyway?

How it applies:

- Heirarchal diagrams of company structures are only ... **diagrams!**

- Each team member must understand their roles and their subsequent responsibilities.

- The job roles and responsibilities must be for the benefit of the organisation, the team and the individual.

- Sometimes it is better to develop the position to suit the personality of the individual rather than find a personality to suit a position ... or

- Sometimes the strength of an individual is not outlined in the job description.

As the Minister for the Sydney Olympics faced the television interviewers over the fiasco of the ticket allocation, he emphasised that it was not his fault. Furthermore, he could not, or would not assign responsibility to anyone within the organisation. So then whose responsibility was it?

Role definitions

How it applies:

- Every member of the team must know and understand **their role**.

- Each member of the team must know and understand the role of every other team member.

- Each team member must understand how all other individual roles and responsibilities combine to facilitate the direction and ultimate success of the team.

- If someone is not carrying out their particular role it is usually because:

  1. They don't understand it.

  2. They don't understand the individual and team benefits of fulfilling their role.

  3. They are too lazy.

A 1994 Commonwealth Games Road cycling team member, Damian McDonald, was asked to describe the role of Australian cycling great Phil Anderson in the 100 km team time trial. He replied: "Phil's job is to get us into a position to win. When he gets us there, us young guys will just go for it!"
The team, consisting of amateurs Damian McDonald, Brett Dennis, Henk Vogels and professional Phil Anderson went on to win the 1994 Commonwealth Games 100 km time trial. Their time would have won the World Championships run the next week.

The team is a tribe

How it applies:

- A tribe can only survive in the wilderness when every member carries out their job and its subsequent responsibilities.

- Some team members will be *"Warriors"*; some will be *"Educators"*; some will be the *"Hunters"*; some will be *"Wise old elders"*, but all will have a significant role to play in the survival of the tribe.

- Ultimately, the survival of the tribe will depend upon the interaction, communication and cooperation between **all members of the tribe.**

In preparation for the 1992 Olympics we decided we were in need of some international experience. On the first trip overseas, there were some new members on the team. One particular member decided, consciously or subconsciously, that he was going to do exactly as he pleased, without following the standards and commitment of the rest of the team.

Having experienced similar situations, I had an idea how the rest of the team would react to this behaviour. I sat back to watch what would unfold. The new team member was late for meetings, would wear the wrong uniform, and would not encourage or congratulate team members on their successes. As I suspected, it didn't take long for the team to reject him and his standards. In effect, the team had removed him from the team process. Ultimately, the new member was the only one of the team who did not swim well. What was worse, though, was that he had totally alienated himself from the group.

By the last day of the meet, however, the new team member had realised the mistake he had made. At the next team meeting he apologised to all members of the team. He then met the coaches and asked permission to swim in the relay teams. We considered that we should allow him this chance, even though he had swum so badly in the individual events. The record books show that he swam a lifetime best to anchor the relay and win the gold medal. More importantly, he had started to rebuild some bridges with the other team members.

When you look upon the team as a tribe, look to see whether each individual contributes, or just consistently takes from the tribe.

Everyone must have a role to play

How it applies:

- Each team member was designated to a certain position (*or were they?*) because they were deemed to be the best for it. Has anything changed? If so, why?

- Every 12 months, get your team members to write out what they currently believe their job roles are, and have they changed in the past 12 months.

- Not everyone in the team is going to have a high profile, be highly paid, or be highly motivated.

- But they are still a valuable team member.

On January 28, 1986, the space shuttle "Challenger", the most technologically advanced piece of machinery in the modern world, exploded because of the loss of resiliency in two $1.50 O-Ring seals.

Everyone's role is critical to the outcome of the team.

Chapter 2

Leadership

"The best leader is the one who has sense
enough to pick good men to do what he wants
done and self-restraint enough to keep from
meddling with them while they do it."
Anonymous

"Real leaders are ordinary people with
extraordinary determination."
Anonymous

Leadership by definition

How it applies:

- Leadership is about people, communication, direction and philosophies.

- Management is about processes and logistics.

- Leaders teach the team commitment.

- Others force results through coercion and look upon that as their strength.

- Great teams operate under great leadership with commitment to the common goal.

- Leaders earn respect through credibility, honesty, trust and loyalty.

- Others demand and coerce respect. (But do they really get it?).

If you read about, or speak to, anyone who has had the opportunity to work with or for a great leader, there is never the problem of too much work. Comments such as "they pushed me too hard" or "they never listened to what we said", or "they never did anything we put forward", do not enter into the equation.

Being a great leader is about loyalty, mutual trust and respect. It is about the quality of communication, listening to the team, and making the hard decisions, then explaining the reasons.

Former US National Security Adviser and chairman of the Joint Chiefs of Staff, General Colin Powell, summed it up best:

"When debating an issue, loyalty means giving your honest opinion, whether you think I will like it or not. Disagreement at this stage stimulates me. But once a decision has been made the debate ends. From that point on loyalty means executing that decision as if it were your own."

Do we lead from the front or from the top?

How this applies:

- The team leader doesn't need to be in charge - but must be out in front!

- Every group must have someone in charge but this person does not have to be the leader.

- When choosing a leader, look to see to whom in the team people naturally gravitate. It's these people from whom they want direction.

- Put your leaders in positions where they can be the most effective.

Rugby League folklore was made when the Newcastle Knights came from behind to win the 1997 ARL Grand Final. Manly had beaten Newcastle 11 consecutive times before that game.

Paul Harragon ("The Chief"), the captain of the Newcastle Knights, called a team meeting the night before the match. He asked each player to say what it would mean to them to win the Grand Final. It was obviously an emotional meeting.

In the dressing room before the Grand Final, Harragon announced that he was going to push the opposition into submission, and that he would show his fellow teammates how to win the game. "I will play in an absolute frenzy. The more the game goes on, the harder I'm going to hit them. I'm not going back to Newcastle a loser." And he didn't!

Sell the ownership of the team to the team

How it applies:

- For any team to move forward it must have direction, leadership **and motivation**.

- Effective motivation will only occur when the team has ownership of the outcome.

- Giving the team input into the vision, strategy and implementation of the project or task creates ownership.

- Ownership can also move to a financial involvement as well.

- Ownership doesn't mean that everyone becomes all things to all people.

- The bottom-line is: all team members need to feel and look at the team **as our team**. Not look at the boss or the captain or whoever is in charge and refer to the team as that person's team.

Day 3, 1996 Atlanta Olympics

The Australian press had begun the onslaught on the Australian Swimming Team. The swimmers cannot start and cannot turn correctly; the coaches have not done a good enough job in preparing them.

Rather than place the blame on someone else or accept that they were not good enough, the swimmers hold a team meeting and discuss a number of issues past, present and future. No coaches, no staff, no Olympic support team, just the swimmers.

They took ownership of the team, they accepted the responsibility of making change, and they took accountability for the outcomes they were after. They were not prepared to accept second best.

This is the type of action that distinguishes a great team from a good team.

What do all great leaders have in common?

How it applies:

They

- Clearly understand the vision.

- Constantly communicate with all the team.

- Are truthful in their approach to all their activities.

- Act when the situation demands action.

- Are passionate about the team and the goal.

- Take risks when the situation calls for it.

- Above all else, they walk the talk.

On his visit to Australia in 1999 General Schwarzkopf, the leader of the Allies in Operation Desert Storm against Iraq in 1990, said: "Leaders are made, not born. You can train your people to be leaders."

On the opposite page are qualities found in good leaders. These qualities can all be acquired.

Chapter 3

Environment

"Some people walk in the
rain - others just get wet!"
Roger Miller

Understand your environment

How it applies:

- We all operate better, are more productive and are prepared to give more when we feel comfortable in the environment in which we operate.

- Research has shown people are happier and more productive when there are challenges that match the individual's skills.

- That they are given a certain amount of ownership in the execution of that challenge.

- That the aesthetic surroundings are not that important as long as they are clean and support the level and direction of the organisation.

- That there are clearly defined goals and unambiguous feedback.

- That there is harmony, direction and commitment within the environment.

- And there are few distractions from the pursuit of said outcome.

- Research has also shown it's not what we do, but how we do it and who we do it with that gives us a sense of satisfaction and attainment.

"Our aim is not to produce champions but to create an environment from whence champions are inevitable."

Legendary Australian Swimming Coach - Forbes Carlile.

Be better than your competition in at least one thing

How it applies:

- Not every team can be the best in everything it does.

- As a group, identify your strengths and weaknesses and work to get better at both.

- Give your team the initial goal of being better at one thing than every other competitor.

- Then be better at two things, then three, then ...?

- To some, being the best at one thing can be the most rewarding experience of their life.

- As an organisation, be part of the process which affords your team members the opportunity to be successful.

- Remember, the road to success begins with one small step.

As a young man learning the skills of tennis. Andre Agassi worked tirelessly every day on all his shots. However, his father had realised that Andre was probably not going to be the biggest or tallest player on the circuit. And tennis was beginning to evolve into the power game that it is today.

He decided that if Andre was going to be competitive he needed "to be able to be involved in the game". After every workout, regardless of what had been previously covered and accomplished, Andre would spend further time working on his return of service.

When we look at all the great "servers" in the world of tennis you begin to judge their strength when they play the service return of Andre Agassi. He has become one of the benchmarks. And the rest of his game is not too bad either!

***

Michael Jordan was cut from his high school basketball team at 15. When he first joined the NBA he was told he was one-dimensional in his offence as he could only slam-dunk. To become a better and more balanced player, Jordan worked emphatically on other areas of his offence. The critics persisted: "He is only an offensive player." So then he worked on his defence. What Michael Jordan contributed to basketball and for sport in general is well documented. He had created a basketball machine, one step at a time.

Leave your ego at the front door

How it applies:

- If you are participating or competing for the benefit of you, then the team is going to suffer.

- Be proud of what the team achieves. And be proud of your role in achieving that outcome.

- In every situation I have seen the individual has always been better because of the people around them.

- Don't let your own publicity or perception get in the way of a great team result.

One of the first tasks basketball coach Phil Jackson had to undertake when he took over coaching the Chicago Bulls in 1989 was to get the highly talented and supremely self-confident Michael Jordan to put his individual goals to one side so the "team's" full potential and energy could be unleashed. As a more experienced player, Michael understood that when you replace the "me" for the "we" in a team situation, the team can go from "good" to "great". And he definitely wanted to get associated with a great team not just a good one.

The record books show that the Chicago Bulls were definitely one of the "great" teams of world sport.

Team success must be preceded by team acceptance of the process to achieve the outcome

How it applies:

- All the strategies and visions in the world will count for nothing if the team doesn't accept the process to achieve that strategy or vision.

- Once the team has agreed to the goal, the next step is to make sure all members accept, support and believe in the process that is to be implemented to achieve the goals.

- Give the team input into the creation of the process or at least into commenting on the process before the implementation.

- Remember the team must accept and believe in the process as if it were its own.

At the Australian Institute of Sport we would often have visitors coming to train with our program.

On one occasion, we had a visitor who continually pulled on the lane lines when swimming backstroke - not a great indiscretion but something that we as a team had decided was unacceptable. I, therefore, took our visitor aside and told him that his actions did not conform to the standards of the team. After only one session he returned to his bad habit.

I told him to get out of the pool, explained that I had been patient, and warned him that if it happened again, he would have to leave. The next day, after removing him from the pool for again pulling on the lane lines, I booked a flight home for our visitor. As he was getting changed, I heard an argument coming from the men's locker room. I went to investigate, and found one of the senior members of the team having a heated argument with the visitor.

After the visitor had left I asked the senior team member what had happened. He explained that the visitor was complaining about the absurd standards and level of commitment the coach required from the team. The senior member had emphasised that it wasn't just the coach's standards, it was also the team's standards. If visitors wanted to be part of the team they had to match the standards.

Evolution of team maturity

How it applies:

- Stage 1
  A group of individuals
  (The feeling of I).

- Stage 2
  A group of individuals with individual goals which have
  commonalities from team member to team member
  (The understanding of us).

- Stage 3
  A team of individuals with common goals, roles and
  responsibilities
  (A team of champions).

- Stage 4
  A team with acceptance of what is required from each team
  member both individually and collectively
  (The belief of us).

- Stage 5
  A team with ownership of its rules, responsibilities and of
  what needs to be done
  (The ownership of we).

A Champion Team

These qualities are not unique to any particular team. If you look at any successful team the majority, if not all, of these qualities would evolve as the team developed and matured.

On the other hand, if you have had contact with teams that have been less than successful, look at the team's developmental process. What part of that process was missing, and how difficult would it have been to include aspects which would have contributed to the qualities which lead to success?

Teams are like plants - they are either growing or they are dying.

Of recent times, Australian politics observed the creation and development of Pauline Hanson's "One Nation" party. In its early days it was surrounded by criticism for some of it policies and the outspoken statements of its leaders. However, throughout all this, it began to rapidly grow and gain support in certain areas. It is presently fighting the courts in relation to the registration of the party etc. As quickly as the party grew, its decline has been even faster.

The 'us and them' mentality

How it applies:

- A lot of teams develop a "them and us" syndrome with the administration.

- The team on the field or at the coalface often sees management as the opposition.

- A clear defining and communicating of roles and responsibilities helps rectify this situation.

- The administrators and managers should be seen as the people to get done what needs to be done to complement the people on the field.

- Communication, communication, and more communication is critical to creating unity.

"The committee needs to understand one thing - I see our role as supporting and complimenting Bill as head coach, and the rest of the coaching staff. If they need something done which would result in our swimmers going faster, then it our job to see that it gets done."

Mr Adrian Gardner, President, Melbourne Vicentre Swimming Club 1994-1997

Relationships within the team

How it applies

- The old days of "loyalty" or being in a team for many years is generally a thing of the past.

- These days, people are less likely to trust, because of downsizing, redirection, cost cutting etc.

- The qualities for relationships within a team are, and should be, transferable to wherever you are.

- Within any team structure there will always be some level of conflict between members.

- Rivalry maybe caused by:

- Superior performance.

- Social rivalry.

- Misunderstanding of goals and responsibilities.

- Lack of space in which to operate.

- Grouping or structure of team members.

- Before making judgment on what course of action to take when looking at relations within the team, look at all the reasons why this may have come about, and who played what role in the scenario. Once you have all the details, then make your move.

*"Be the type of player that the person standing
beside you wants to play with."*
Newcastle Knights NRL players' motto.

***

*"Chief, you are a truly great person and you
were a truly great player, and it dawned on me
on Friday night that I am going to be privileged
to be able to say to my kids that I played with
Paul Harragon."*
**Newcastle Knights Five Eight
Mathew Johns
Newcastle Morning Herald
May 30, 1999**

Personalities or positions - what comes first?

How it applies:

- First, define your team structure in terms of positions needed and/or wanted.

- Second, where you want to retain team members, orientate the position to suit the individual style of the team member.

- Sometimes this is not possible, but in most cases you can get very close to the mark.

- It is easier to change a job description and position for someone who brings food to the table of the team each day, than to change the person to suit the position.

- Always look at the individual's strengths and weaknesses and ask where do they best suit our needs.

*Many times people with extraordinary skills
have not been given an opportunity because
they didn't fit the description of the job offered.
Take, for example, the following people:*

*Oprah Winfrey couldn't get into TV because
people in the industry believed she didn't have
the right look.*

*Steven Spielberg was told he wasn't suitable for
film school. He learned his trade by sneaking
into studios and watching other directors.*

*Jacques Cousteau wanted to be an astronaut
but had broken both his arms, which made him
ineligible to join a space program. One day,
while watching spiders submerging in their air
bubble, he brainstormed the idea that became
the aqualung.*

Always look at what the individual has to offer!

Chapter 4

Communication

"A single conversation across a table with a
wise man is worth a month's study of books."
Chinese Proverb

"Whenever we communicate with each other
correctly there is an exchange of energy."
Reshad Feild

Up, down, sideways - it's all critical

How it applies:

- Communication is singularly the most important ingredient that has to be conquered for the success of the team.

- For communication to be successful, it must be a two-way street. From management out to the front line and from the front line back to the management.

- For ownership in the team to occur, the team must feel it is able to convey its thoughts and ideas back to management without fear of being isolated or persecuted.

- Management must ensure its communication channels to the front line are not filtered and should always ensure it has several mechanisms to guarantee unfiltered communication is occurring.

- Smart management teams spend a lot of time talking to the front line and the customers. They conduct regular staff surveys and attend team meetings where they shut up and listen.

- Every business should conduct an annual communication audit just as they conduct a financial end-of-year audit.

During my six years at the Australian Institute of Sport, I would try, every Friday, to go around to the administration offices and say "Hi" to everyone. One of my most important weekly visits was to then executive director Rob de Castella. My reason for these visits was to maintain a solid and successful working relationship.

Because of this relationship which had developed, Rob and I could meet with no barriers to inhibit our communication.

Face to face

How it applies:

- One of the foundations of good team relationships is face-to-face communication - and not just when it is necessary to be with the team.

- The communication does not have to be in-depth but it must be sincere.

- It can be as simple as taking the time to walk up to someone, extend your hand and say "Hi".

- Acknowledgment is the highest form of flattery.

- Everyone loves to be acknowledged and kept up to date.

- Face-to-face communication allows you to get feedback from the receiver.

- It also allows the sender to see how the communication is being received.

In 1991, I had the pleasure of coaching Brent Harding at the Australian Institute of Sport. Brent had been selected in both the Pan Pacific Championship team and the World Student Games team. The World Student Games were in Sheffield, England and the Pan Pacs were in Edmonton, Canada two-and-a-half weeks later. Australian Swimming had a policy which did not allow swimmers to participate in major international meets, which were close in time.

I called national head coach, Don Talbot, to see if an exception could be made in Brent Harding's case. I had hoped to resolve the problem by phone, but during the conversation Don said he would prefer to discuss the matter face to face.

When Don arrived in Canberra the following week, I proceeded to state the practicalities and strategies behind my request. I got the first, second and third degrees, but in the end Don agreed to let Brent compete in both meets.

Some years later I asked Don the reason why he wanted to have the discussion face to face. He told me that he wanted to hear my reasoning, and see if I was passionate in what I believed was best for Brent.

Listen, learn and then speak

How it applies:

- Communication is more than just talking to someone. It is about taking the time to listen, to understand, to presenting your point of view and to be able to discuss things openly.

- As Stephen Covey pointed out in his book *The 7 Habits of Highly Effective people*", first we must understand and then be understood.

- When two people have differing views in the team, several roadblocks can occur to excellent communication.

  1. Neither party listens to the other.

  2. Each is insistent on getting their point of view across.

  3. Neither takes the time to think and feel what the other person is feeling or trying to achieve.

  4. Sometimes one party will make assumptions about the knowledge of the other, which is, in fact, quite wrong.

- Remember, at the completion of any discussion, if the parties don't agree they should at least understand the other's position.

My mother once said to me:
"When you are born, people
spend the first few years teaching
you how to walk and talk, then
the next few years teaching you
how to read and write. But when
does anyone teach you how to
listen?"

Other forms of communication - e-mails, letters, faxes, phones - when do you use what.

How it applies:

- Face to face with someone is always the best form of communication.

- The next best form is the phone and after that take your pick.

- If you are working together, it is imperative to be able to look, see and hear not what someone is saying but how they say it. Do they really believe it? Is it something they are passionate about?

- It is always a lot easier to say "no" to an e-mail or fax.

- However, the advantages of written communication are that it is portable and can be reviewed in detail.

- Sometimes the easiest form of communication will not be the best. <u>Be very careful when selecting the easiest option.</u>

- The success of what you are trying to communicate, regardless of the form you present it in, will be dependent on several things:

1. Your association with the recipient.

2. Your credibility with the recipient.

3. An opening statement or attention-grabber.

4. How long you can maintain their interest?

A good friend, who is a highly respected basketball coach in the US, wanted to sell tickets to an upcoming event which was to be held in a university town and which had been given little publicity. He had posters made which simply said: "Who Knows?" The posters were widely erected overnight but were only on display for the one day.

The next day, students were asking: "Who knows what?" The coach then arranged for people to walk around in T-shirts that said: "Ask me, I know." However, the only thing they were allowed to tell the student was: "October 22." The coach's next move was to have people phoning everyone they could and say: "October 22, 6 pm, basketball hall." At 6 pm, on October 22, 6000 students and staff turned up to find out what this secrecy was all about.

When the spectators arrived they found the room was empty except for a single microphone in the middle of the court. At 6 pm sharp the coach walked on to the court, introduced himself and each member of his team and staff. He then announced that their first game would be held on November 3 and tickets to the game were now on sale.

The imaginative publicity scheme paid off - it was, of course, a sell-out home game.

Body language

How it applies:

- It has often been said it's not what you say but how you say it.

- The same thing applies to body language.

- How you act, or how you walk and what you say can sometimes send mixed messages.

- Our mannerisms and facial expressions portray messages about us and how we feel.

- Be careful.

- People will place more belief in non-verbal messages, because it is easier to hide the truth in verbal messages.

- Great teams know how to read team members.

- And then how and when to give each other space.

- This is a learned skill and a must for all successful team members.

- As often as possible keep all your forms of communication upbeat and positive.

Over the years, there have been many great stories about athletes and their ability to out-perform their rivals under any circumstance. One of my favourites is about the great Canadian swimmer Alex Baumann.

At the 1986 World Championships, Alex contracted a virus and was ill when the meet started. He was so ill that, in the 400 individual medley, the event for which he held the world record, he was the second last qualifier for the final. As is customary at major international meets, all the finalists were individually announced. As Alex's name was announced he was overcome with sickness and proceeded to be ill in a container behind the block.

Officials came to his aid and asked if he wanted to continue. Alex replied: "Of course."

Many years later, I had the opportunity to spend some time with Alex and finally got the chance to ask him why he had continued to swim that night when he was so ill and knew he probably couldn't win. He replied: "I wanted to show my competitors that I was going to be tough to beat when I was ill, but impossible to beat when I was well."

Incidentally, Alex Baumann won a bronze medal in the 400 individual medley that night at the 1986 World Championships.

Being able to tell each other what we really think

How it applies:

- One of the great things a team needs is to be able to pinpoint weaknesses and then openly discuss them.

- Sometimes people are reluctant to say what they feel for fear of upsetting someone.

- Great teams understand that for weaknesses to become strengths they need to be identified and discussed.

- A weakness will always remain a weakness if it isn't discussed openly and with conviction.

- I don't think that these discussions should become a free-for-all.

- But if people understand it is the situation or a person's actions that are being discussed and not an individual or their personality.

- Then things can, and will, proceed.

- In the beginning, this will take a lot of work and open-mindedness from members of the team to accept this form of communication.

In my experience, when dealing with sporting teams, relationships are not always strong enough to allow constructive criticism. This can lead to members becoming hurt and upset. It is important for team members to understand that the coach is not attacking the individual, but a situation. However, each individual has to accept a certain amount of responsibility for that situation.

The team members have to be strong enough to accept that, in order to work towards their goal, they need to be able to speak freely to each other without anyone taking offence.

A National Basketball League team, the South-East Melbourne Magic, was strong enough to allow this process to take place. It is the best team I have seen.

If you want the accolades for the successes be prepared to accept the criticism for the losses. It's called accountability.

Process to handle problems and conflict

How it applies:

- While mediation is fine, there will be times when confrontation is needed.

- The process that I have used to handle problems and conflict within the teams I have worked with are as follows:

  1. Identify the problem.

  2. Discuss and analyse the issues (this takes an open mind).

  3. Develop the strategies to solve the problems.

  4. Instigate strategy.

  5. Monitor effectiveness of the strategy.

  6. Go back to number one, if needed.

- Involve the team in the solution.

Not long after I started work at the Australian Institute of Sport I became involved in a heated discussion with one of the swimmers. I told him what I thought were his problems as a swimmer, and he then told me what he considered were my shortcomings as a coach. Not a great start to a good working relationship!

Over the next week we both thought about the future. The fact was that neither of us was going to leave, so we had better find some common ground.

We took some time, got to know one another, and spoke about our problems. Together we developed plans and strategies for the future, and both worked hard towards achieving their intended outcomes.

Even though our relationship had a rocky start, there were benefits. Because we were prepared to discuss our differences and to start afresh, mutual trust and respect led to the development of a great athlete/coach relationship. Although this swimmer has now retired, and I have moved on, we still remain great friends.

Thanks to
Martin Roberts
Dual Olympian
Triple Commonwealth Games gold medallist
World Student Games Double gold medallist.

The home-ground advantage

How it applies:

- Equally important in terms of effectiveness of communication is the venue.

- If you have the same type of meeting in the same venue all of the time.

- The team members will just say: "Oh, here we go again."

- Pick venues and sites that are supportive and in line with the type of meeting you want to have.

- The venue will also help pre-empt the type of meeting and get the group's mind on the job.

Over the years I have conducted many
meetings for various reasons, using appropriate
venues to suit the occasion. Some examples are
as follows:

1. General meetings – A general purpose room.
2. Feel-good meeting – Outside, in a park, or at
the beach.
3. Kick in the pants, Team – The locker room.
4. Kick in the pants, Individual – My office.
5. Important individual meetings – A venue
where I know the athlete will feel comfortable.

Chapter 5

Goals

"Obstacles are those frightful things you see
when you take your eyes off your goals."
Anonymous

Creating the direction or where we are going

How it applies:

- Within in any team, someone is ultimately responsible for creating the direction.

- The more that direction is pushed down in small amounts, the more the next level can take ownership and plan its direction within the outlines set by the level above.

- Then everyone takes ownership.

- Everyone travels a common road.

- It is always better to have your hands on the steering wheel, than to be a navigator in a car that crashes.

Every team must have a plan to guide it towards its desired outcome. Having a plan is one thing, but keeping to that plan is more difficult. Sometimes we let the short-term result blind our vision of the long-term goal.

Over the years I have seen the careers of many outstanding young swimmers destroyed because the people around them were not interested in long-term development. The swimmer's supporters cannot see beyond the 12-year-old champion. Coaches are changed frequently to achieve short-term results. However, focusing on short-term results will not allow for a long-term plan that would ultimately provide the benefits.

When a plan is developed it must include checking mechanisms. The plan needs to be overviewed, questioned and, if needed, modified. It must also be given the opportunity to be implemented and the time to be completed.

Faith is admirable; blind faith is stupidity. A plan should never be followed blindly.

Individual goals in a team environment

How it applies:

- It would be ridiculous to assume that everyone will come to work just for the betterment of the company or the team.

- Everyone has wants and needs.

- To some it will be financial, friendship, sense of worth, notoriety.

- The secret to team goals is to make sure that individual goals are aligned to the team goal.

- Communication, validation of feelings and mutual respect will highlight the individual wants and needs of team members.

The goal of the 1994 Commonwealth Games swimming team was to win every event on the program. For this to happen, it needed every swimmer to reach their own individual goal by trying to win their individual events.

Achieving individual goals leads to the completion of the team goals. One does not cancel out the other.

Australia won 34 gold medals, 20 silver medals, 11 bronze medals at the 1994 Commonwealth Games. It won every event on days two, three and six.

Risks - calculated or careless?

How it applies:

- Sometimes the most motivating and productive times of our lives is when we are out of our comfort zone.

- Careless, non-rehearsed, badly planned risks, should not be mistaken for calculated, well thought out, "Have a go" attitudes.

- In everything we do there is both calculated and careless risk.

- How the percentage of this works out is dependent on every situation and every individual mindset and motivation.

Jerry Seinfeld, after the completion of the last episode of "Seinfeld", was asked when was the happiest time of his life. He replied:

"Right now. I suppose I bet on myself and didn't lose. And that can be a pretty rewarding experience."

Simpler not simple

How it applies:

- Goals can be as simple as you want them to be or as complex as you need them to be.

- Because they are basic doesn't mean they don't have substance or direction.

- Be wary of the old adage "paralysis by analysis".

- But the key is to know what it is you really want?

- And then devise the goals and plans that suit the orientation and strength of the individual team members and the team.

In response to the question
"How did you set goals to win
four successive Olympic gold
medals?" US discuss thrower Al
Oerter replied:

"After each training session, if I
had trained well, I would mark
the calendar. After each year I
would have 365 marks. At the
end of each Olympiad, I would
have 1400 marks. I knew my
standards for those marks. So I
knew I would be tough to beat."

Mission statements

How it applies:

- There are as many different ways to come up with mission statements as there are mission statements.

- For a mission statement to have credibility and significance.

- It must be made up with input from all team members.

- The mission statement must be a reflection of the group.

- The mission statement is the thing that keeps the team together when things get tough.

- The members of the team should be able to recite it or, at the very worst, be able to relate to its origin, its meaning and the direction it gives.

Recently, at my local bank, I noticed that, sitting on the teller's counter, was the organisation's mission statement. It was beautifully worded and well presented in a nice perspex frame. Covering it with my hand, I asked the teller to recite the statement to me. Somewhat embarrassed, the teller admitted not knowing even a single line of the mission statement, although she did have some recollection of the meaning of it.

Chapter 6

Rules by Which We Live

"The highest reward for a person's toil is not
what they get for it but what
they become by it."
John Ruskin

"We all find occasions where we have to
choose between what we believe is right and
what we suspect is advantageous."
Sam Edwin Jnr

Development of a culture

How it applies:

- We talk about personalities; we talk about goals long-term and short-term; we talk about mission statements.

- In all this we are manufacturing direction and standards.

- But, in its simplest form, all this is creating a culture.

- And the thing about culture is that, in the early years, people are going to have be prepared to be open-minded and teachable.

- Creating a culture is about standards, ethics, commitment etc.

- But developing true culture is about time-lining so the culture becomes autocratic.

- People support, communicate, and deliver the culture of the team in everything that they do.

- The team become a representation of the culture and the culture a representation of the team.

In the early 1990s, Australian Swimming brought in a dry (no alcohol) policy for all its teams. Initially, this policy was met with great resentment from the older swimmers and the coaches, who considered they were old enough to make their own decisions. Nevertheless, the rule stood.

Today, the rule is no longer a problem for anyone associated with the team. In fact, it is probably worn like a badge of courage by most, showing the international swimming fraternity the sacrifices Australian swimmers are prepared to make, to be the best.

At first, it was not an easy process getting everyone to agree to the policy, but in hindsight it was a great decision.

Standards

How it applies:

- In almost every case I have been involved with, you can set the bar or standard at whatever height you want.

- The secret is not the height of the bar or the standards being pursued.

- The secret is to get the team to pursue the standard or the height of the bar.

- And to be committed to that pursuit.

- My belief is Australians will go after anything if it is presented to them in the right manner and the pitfalls and benefits are outlined.

- And the individuals involved understand the benefits to them, the team and the organisation.

A reporter once asked me to describe my coaching style. I replied: "Intolerant."

"That is a pretty ordinary answer for someone who works on a daily basis with young people," he said.

"Not intolerant of them," I said, *"but whatever I tolerate, they will be happy with. So I must be intolerant for them, so they can reach the standards necessary for their own individual successes."*

Philosophies

How it applies:

• A philosophy is basically a set of principles or guidelines which direct the team in practical-type situations.

• A philosophy will only be as strong as the amount of time and effort that goes into creating it.

• A strong philosophy will allow you consistency in direction and decisions.

• Your philosophy becomes your trademark when dealing with people and situations.

• Quality is important.

The background to my coaching philosophy is easy.

Each individual has a certain amount of ability. It is my job to get them to acknowledge, to understand and to respect that ability. Every day they must do what they can to maximise that ability without compromise.

Ethics

How it applies:

- Sometimes it is very difficult to make ethical decisions.

- You have to take into consideration economic, social and professional pressures.

- Which sometimes directly oppose the situation.

- The making of the ethical decision will please some and upset others.

- These are real issues that need to be looked at well in advance.

- As they probably will not go away with time.

- Any decision that is made will reflect on the decision-makers' sensitivity and commitment to ethics.

- It is far more important to consider the right thing to do, than what you have the right to do.

Rule 13

"When in charge take control"

Rule 14

"Do what is right"

General H Norman Schwarzkopf.

Morals

How it applies:

- The term morals describes beliefs, customs and traditions that are reflected in personal convictions about what is right and wrong.

- Everyone has a set of rules by which they live and this becomes their values or morals.

- In a team situation we must learn to accept these values and morals into the team.

- But at the same time individuals must understand that, for the team benefit and harmony, they should not try to enforce their own personal morality or values on others.

- These morals and values have a huge impact on the attitudes and beliefs which can influence and create certain behaviours.

- This needs to be understood and incorporated into the makeup of the team.

"The quality of a man's life is in direct proportion to his commitment to excellence - regardless of his chosen field of endeavour."
Coach Vince Lombardi

Chapter 7

Motivation

"Desire is the key to motivation, but it's the determination and commitment to an unrelenting pursuit of your goal – a commitment to excellence – that will enable you to attain the success you seek."

Mario Andretti

Never Give Up

How it applies:

In his book titled *Never Give Up*, Graeme Alford outlines the process he went through while in Pentridge to rebuild his life. These are Graeme's key points on how to "never give up".

- No matter how bad it is, you have to keep going.

- You are never a failure until you concede defeat.

- Persistence prevails when all else fails.

First Proposal ... No
Second Proposal ... No
Third Proposal ... No
Fourth Proposal...No
Fifth Proposal ... Send me a tour itinerary
Sixth Proposal ... Send me a
more detailed itinerary.
Seventh Proposal ... No. The tour is too hard.
A personal letter ... Yes

This was the 12-month process World Masters
of Business organiser Graeme Alford went
through to sign Lee Iacocca to visit Australia in
1997.

Not a part-time thing but a lifetime thing

How it applies:

- Being motivated doesn't mean when things get hard that you don't get down on the situation.

- But being motivated means that, through the rollercoaster ride of life, we don't take our mind off the bigger picture.

- Motivation is something that we usually associate with the things we like to do.

- Motivation should be attached to everything we do in life.

In 1993, the Australian Institute of Sport (AIS) decided to restructure the swimming program. Part of that restructure was to move away from a separate men's and women's team.

Because of this restructure, I took over coaching some of the women distance swimmers from my good friend Dr Ralph Richards. One of those swimmers was Chloe Flutter, from Canberra. Initially, Chloe's opinions on the way she should train did not coincide with mine. We both worked hard to find common ground.

While I was in America, Chloe snapped the biceps tendon in her arm. The doctors reattached it by drilling a hole in the bone and fixing the tendon through the hole. Because of this operation, Chloe spend quite some time out of the water. AIS scholarships are awarded on performance and so Chloe was given the ultimatum to swim fast or lose the scholarship. We tried several different training strategies until finally, on her last chance at a meet in Melbourne, Chloe came through with a best time.

Through all this, she continued with her university studies. When I moved to Melbourne, Chloe came down and joined our squad, and we continued to work as a team on her swimming, her pursuit of her academic goals and her direction in life.

I was extremely proud when, in 1998, I picked up the newspaper to see a photo of Chloe Flutter after she had been awarded a Rhodes scholarship.

Motivation is internal not external

How it applies:

- You can use external means to help lift you in certain situations.

- But the bottom line is you have to be prepared to make changes to enjoy or be motivated by a situation.

- Perception is the key to enjoyment.

- How you look at things and how that makes you feel, has a great effect on your motivation.

- Is the glass half empty or half full?

I have been asked many times to speak to teams, businesses and sporting organisations. When I ask what I should talk about, in 90 per cent of cases the response is the same: "Be motivational."

You can tell of your own experiences, outline situations, or tell stories that are both interesting and humorous. For the speech to be motivational, however, the individual must accept it as being that way. That is why motivation is an internal reaction that may be aided by an external situation.

Playing for something bigger than you

How it applies:

- If you just participate for your own satisfaction, when things get hard it is too easy to walk away.

- I think getting personal satisfaction from the things we do is a must.

- But we do not always like the things we have to do.

- As an individual or team you must find that "greater thing".

- It will be your guiding light through the journey of success.

"What does this football jumper mean to you?

Does it represent the history of one of the league's proudest and most respected teams? Does it represent the opportunity to play the game you love? Does it represent the opportunity of an income?

Or does it represent the commitment, desire and dedication of this team of people who sit here before me?

You must decide the answer to these questions.

I can tell you one thing. It must mean something to you - and you must play for something greater than yourself."

Part of my address to the Hawthorn Football Club in 1995

Success is a journey not a destination

How it applies:

- Doesn't matter what we do and how successful we are at it - even when you get to the final challenge of that situation and you have succeeded.

- The lessons and skills that you learned along the way only help you and the team to incorporate them into the next challenge at the next level.

- On this journey of success, as in any other journey, there will be a variety of experiences, of terrains and environments.

- As you go along, take time to wind down the window of the Kombi and breathe the air, smell the flowers, look at the magnificent countryside.

- Don't miss the opportunities along the way.

In December 1995, the Australian World Short Course Swimming team (the World Team Champions), visited the NASA Space Centre, in Cape Canaveral, Florida.

"This is the room where we monitored the Apollo 11 moon landing. We will now replay the footage as we saw it live from this room. The voices you will hear are those of the ground staff who stood in this room. They guided the Apollo 11 moon landing and Neil Armstrong's first steps on the lunar surface."
(NASA Tour Guide)

The hairs on my neck stood bolt upright.

Chapter 8

Success

"It's a funny thing about life; if you refuse to
accept anything but the best
you very often get it."
W. Somerset Maugham

"The future belongs to those who believe in
the beauty of their dreams."
Eleanor Roosevelt

Clearly and all times communicate what you mean by success

How it applies:

- History has shown that not everyone can be Prime Minister, Businessperson of the year, Olympic gold medallist or a Rhodes scholar.

- But everyone can be successful in some parts of their life.

- Outline to all members of the team how they will be judged in regard to success.

- But also listen to what they think success is.

- All team members must understand the description of success as it relates to them.

It was 1996, and I had to discuss team and individual goals with members of the Melbourne Vicentre Swimming Club. We had four members of our club going to the Olympics, a further two going to the Paralympics, as well as other team members who were swimming at State, National Age and National Open championships.

Because of the various levels of swimmers, I had to be very careful how, as members of the one team, we were going to judge the success of the group. If I had continually spoken to the group about our impending success at the Olympics, the people who were swimming at State and National level might have sat and wondered how this related to them. It would have been easy for them to think that all I cared about were those going to Atlanta, and that the other members of the group didn't mean anything to me. Nothing could have been further from the truth.

The success of all team members must be judged at all levels of participation. Team members must be told, and must understand the basis on which their success is judged, and the ramifications for any lack of performance.

The winning is in the picking

How it applies:

- I don't think you win competitive situations with strategies, with game plans or with technological breakthroughs.

- You win competitive situations with people.

- Business and sport are the same: put the right people on the paddock and you will win.

- As a coach, a leader, a CEO, people are the greatest resource available to us.

In 1995, the National Basketball League team, South-East Melbourne Magic, signed a player Mike Kelly, from the then Nunawading CBA team.

Kelly had trialled for a number of NBL teams in the years he had spent in Australia after leaving the United States, including the Magic team. When he did try out for the Magic a few seasons before, the needs of the team didn't match what Kelly could offer. However, in 1995, the needs and ability did match and he was a starting player in the latter part of the season.

It soon became obvious that Kelly was a priceless member of the team. He was a tireless worker and a positive, upbeat and likeable guy. He gave respect and received it from all those who met him. He was not overly talented, but this was made up tenfold by his desire, commitment and self-discipline.

As a player, Mike Kelly went from strength to strength, as did the Magic team. In 1996, the South-East Melbourne Magic was crowned NBL champions and Mike Kelly was named Most Valuable Player of the playoff series.

Earning respect

How it applies:

- Everyone wants acceptance for who they are and what they do.

- Acknowledgment of what we do is important.

- Acknowledgment and admiration for what we do is more important.

- Respect for what we do and how we do it is the ultimate success.

Most people have had an opportunity, whether it is in business, sport, or life in general, to observe and participate in events which have involved very successful people.

Even though someone is successful, it does not mean they receive our respect. The reason for the lack of respect may be that the success has come from a "win at all costs" attitude, which has gone against our belief of fair play and sportsmanship. Respect is also lost when a successful person is rude or obnoxious.

The people we admire the most are those people who have earned our respect, not only for what they have done, but also for how they have done it.

People don't come to your funeral because you were successful; they don't come because you were rich; they come out of respect.

Everyone must contribute for the glory of all

How it applies:

- We are all human and the thing that drives us most is personal satisfaction.

- We have spent a few pages going over the elements of teamwork.

- In the end the strength and standard of the team will be highlighted when individual wants and needs are removed.

- If the teams direction, standards, philosophies and goals have been

  1. Clearly thought out

  2. Clearly communicated

  3. Clearly understood

  4. And the team takes ownership

- Then, and only then, will the team members put aside individual agendas to help the TEAM reach its prescribed outcomes.

When I informed Chris Fydler that he would
not be swimming in the 1996 Olympic medley
relay team, this was his response:

"In the 1992 Barcelona Olympics I was part of
the original 4 x 100 medley relay team with
Tom Stachewicz, Phil Rogers and Jon Seiben.
We became known as the 'Deadly Medley'. I
have been part of that team and swum in every
major meet since. I have seen us go from
nowhere to Commonwealth Games
Champions in 1994 to today, where we have
the chance to win an Olympic medal. I am not
swimming well enough to be selected on the
team today and I understand that, but I am still
part of this team and today we will win an
Olympic medal."

The team (Steven Dewick, Phil Rogers, Scott
Miller, and Michael Klim) went on to win a
bronze medal in Atlanta and also won a gold
medal at the 1998 Perth World Championships
(Matt Welsh, Phil Rogers, Michael Klim, Chris
Fydler).

Chris Fydler was a 1992, 1996 and 2000
Olympian, and one of our finest athletes.

Their life is better for the experience

How it applies:

- When team members eventually depart the team and they will.

- For a multitude of reasons.

- You would like them to look at the time they spent with the team and say:

- I am a better person for the experience of being in that team.

- This maybe because you won. They learned more about the processes. They were respected for who they are, the relationships they had. It was fun.

- The team should offer and deliver more than just its primary purpose.

My primary job description at the Australian
Institute of Sport was to get members of the
team to swim faster and contribute to the
international success of the AIS swimming
program. However, during the six years I spent
at the Institute, I brought to Canberra some
young people aged between 16 and 18.

There was a huge duty of care for these young
swimmers. I became not only their coach and
their surrogate parent, but also their
disciplinarian, educator, counsellor and
moneylender. My responsibility also extended
to one of relationship expert.

I look at these swimmers today and take pride
in seeing how they have grown up. I take
pleasure in reading the letters that parents have
written to me thanking me for the role I have
played, not only in developing their children's
swimming, but helping them to grow into fine
young Australians.

At all costs - why not?

How it applies:

- Winning isn't everything; it is the only thing. We have all heard this said and probably said it ourselves in some context.

- At times this is certainly correct - that winning is our primary objective.

- But to win in the essence of fair play, of honesty and in the essence of sportsmanship.

- Then that is truly winning.

- Some may see it differently; well, that is up to them.

At the 1994 World Swimming Championships, Chinese women won 11 of the 13 individual women's events. No one could believe it.

Although those swimmers may still have their medals, some have been stripped of their records. Very few, if any, have the respect of the swimming world.

Yes, they are winners, but at what cost?

Overcoming fear

How it applies:

- In everyone's life there comes opportunities that can, and will have, a significant and positive impact upon it.

- Unfortunately, not all these opportunities are acted on.

- In most cases, we don't act because we always have this fear of failure.

- We must prepare ourselves for these opportunities - by getting out of our comfort zone as often as possible.

- These comfort zone exercises can be as simple as giving up chocolate for a week, to getting up and singing in front of your team mates.

- The more we practise overcoming fear in a variety of circumstances, the better we get at dealing with it.

It's not the critic who counts; not the man who points out how the strong man stumbles, or where the doer of deeds could have done better.

The credit belongs to the man who is actually in the arena, whose face is marred by dust and sweat and blood; who strives valiantly; who errs, and comes short again and again, because there is no effort without error and shortcoming...;

Who knows the great enthusiasms, the great devotions; who spends himself in a worthy cause; who at best knows in the end the triumph of high achievement.

And at worst, if he fails, at least fails while daring greatly, so that his place shall never be with those cold and timid souls who know neither victory nor defeat.

President Theodore Roosevelt
"The Man in the Arena", Paris 1910

The other side of the pursuit of success - the 'Tall Poppy' syndrome"

How it applies:

- You can have a definition of success.

- Have your mission statements and your goals.

- Communicated everything to all concerned.

- Counting down the days to liftoff.

- And the day before the press, your competitors proceed to point out 100 ways why it won't work.

- The "Tall Poppy" syndrome in Australia is alive and well.

- We too often try to pull the opposition down a peg.

- Others do not always support the pursuit of success.

- They would rather see you down at their level than to be "successful".

*One of my teachers said to me on the day I left
year 10 Toronto High School:*

*"Nelson, you are lazy. You will never survive in
the outside world. You will never amount to
anything and you will never work hard enough
to achieve anything."*

*On the day I left Tamworth to return to
Newcastle to prepare a number of swimmers
for the 1988 Seoul Olympics, the parting words
of one of the parents were:*

*"Yeah, go on, think about yourself and no-one
else. Olympics, my bum. I've got more chance
of flying to the moon than you ever have of
being an Olympic coach."*

*This was only an isolated instance. The people
of the Scully Park Swimming Club were
fantastic for the 12 months I worked with them.*

Chapter 9

Live Locally, Think Globally

"Never waste time and energy wishing you
were somewhere else, doing something else.
Accept the situation and realise you are the
way you are, doing what you are doing, for a
very specific reason. Realise that
nothing is by chance."
Eileen Caddy

Stand here; look there

How it applies:

- To so many people, in so many things, the grass always looks greener on the other side of the fence.

- If only I were born at some other time. If only I had his money. If only we had this computer. If only we had this account. If only he had signed with our team not their's.

- Look around for the great ideas but then make them better and put them into your team to make it better.

After the 1991 Perth World Championships, the head coach of the Australian Institute of Sport Swimming Program, Bill Sweetenham, invited Dr Helga Pfeiffer and Dr Harold Tunneman from the East German Sports Institute in Leipzig, to Canberra to visit our program.

We spent three days locked in a room with a translator and a person taking notes. After three days, and reams and reams of notes and diagrams, I looked at Bill Sweetenham and said: "Now we have the answers, let's put this stuff into action."

He looked at me and said: "You haven't learned anything in three years, have you. We don't live in East Germany, so their model is not going to suit us. Let's go through this with a fine tooth comb, work out what is good, develop it to see it at its next stage, and then that's what we put into place."

Our home is where we are

How it applies:

- You live, operate and socialise in a certain environment for certain reasons.

- This is where you live.

- Sometimes the grass always looks greener on the other side of the fence.

- But this is not always true.

- Before spending all your time dreaming about somewhere else.

- Spend some time thinking about how here could be better.

- Make home better first, and then take a look at the real picture.

- Dream if you wish but bring those dreams home.

- And make your dreams a reality.

I realised in 1985 that if I was to become a better coach, I had to gain more experience. I left Newcastle in 1986 to follow my dream of becoming an international swimming coach.

That dream took me to Tamworth for one year, Canberra for six years and Melbourne for three years. There were also numerous overseas trips, including two Olympic Games, two World Championships and a Commonwealth Games. This has provided the opportunity for me to work with some of the greatest names in world sport.

In 1997, the University of Newcastle allowed me the opportunity to bring that dream home again, when we started the University Of Newcastle Swimming program.

Work with what you've got

How it applies:

- Sometimes all of us look for ways to make our lives, our work or our sport easier or better by getting things to help us.

- Sometimes these things do what they are supposed to do, that is, making the situation more productive.

- But do these things really make situations better or do they just make them easier.

- When you work with what you have and you get what you want, you will be a lot happier.

During the 1997 NBL season, two key players for South-East Melbourne Magic, centres John Dorge (211 cms) and Chris Anstey (213 cms), were out of action for various reasons. There were two critical games coming up, one against the Illawarra Hawks in Wollongong and the other against the North Melbourne Giants. No one expected us to win either of the games. As coaching staff, we worked with what we had - a great bunch of guys who wanted to win. We won both games.

Chapter 10

United We Stand, Divided We Fall

"You can make more friends in two months by
becoming interested in other people than you
can in two years by trying to get people
interested in you."
Dale Carnegie

Praise your teammates first

How it applies:

- Egos can be our greatest asset or our greatest undoing.

- A lot depends on how healthy it is and how we use it.

- The greatest destruction of a team is for someone to stand up when questioned about the team success and say the word "I".

- You talk TEAM success; people on the outside will understand your role in that success.

- Your telling people how great you are doesn't necessarily make you good in their eyes.

Following is a conversation between Paul Maley from Channel 10 and John Dorge, the co-captain South-East Melbourne Magic.

Paul Maley: *"The undisputed most valuable player from tonight's game with 28 points 13 rebounds and three blocked shots, John Dorge. John, you've got to be happy with your form this year."*

John Dorge: *"I am happy with my form this year, but the reason I am playing so well is that everyone on this team is playing well. That is because everyone is training hard and putting in the extra effort. We are really bonding well as a team."*

Paul Maley: *"Just watching the game, it is so apparent the chemistry of this team. It is a pleasure to watch and for you it must be fun to play."*

John Dorge: *"We are enjoying the type of basketball we are playing, but I can assure you, it has come from a lot of hard work."*

Also Australian Wallaby Captain John Eales interview after kicking the winning goal in the second game of the 2000 Bledisloe Cup.

Respect for teammates

How it applies:

- Relationships on any team should be based on honesty, loyalty and mutual respect.

- I don't think that it is necessary for everyone on the team to be the best of friends.

- But I do believe for the team to work effectively, there must be mutual respect.

- But within all relationships, within a team, there should be some element of friendship.

The Chicago Bulls NBA basketball team won an amazing six NBA Championships. Much of the credit for those wins was attributed to Michael Jordan, arguably the greatest basketballer of all time.

During one of the playoff series, with very little time on the clock, Jordan had a chance to score the winning shot and so win that year's championship. Instead of shooting, Jordan passed the ball to Steve Kerr, who missed the shot and allowed the opposition to win the game. This put the opposition back into the race for the NBA Championship.

It eventually came down to the final game of the playoff series. Everyone assumed that, if the game was tight, Jordan would take the final shot to secure victory. However, Jordan simply did what he had done before: he passed the ball to Steve Kerr who this time made sure he hit the winning shot.

When interviewed after the game, Jordan was asked why he passed the ball to Kerr who, last time, had cost them the game. Jordan replied that the team had faith in Steve Kerr, but after missing the last shot, Steve didn't believe in himself. Jordan said he just wanted to show Steve that the team members still believed in him.

Trust in other people within the organisation

How it applies

- In sport, athletes learn very early to put trust in people they don't really know that well.

- Although, with the advent of professionalism and money.

- The days of trust are a little harder to come by.

- How can you trust someone that at the end of the season might trade you?

- Business is very similar - downsizing, cut-backs, restructuring.

- All lends itself to lack of trust.

- Understand the realities of the modern times.

- Trust people on what you see, what you hear and what they give.

- A lot of great decisions (and a few bad ones) have come from the old gut decision.

- Basically, we all understand when we are being looked after and when we are not.

"Ever put your life in another man's hands and ask him to put his life in yours?"
Jack Nicholson
"A Few Good Men"

A champion team or a team of champions

How it applies:

- One is not right and the other wrong.

- But if you are heading forward as a team.

- Then a champion team is the title you want.

- Individual brilliance is fantastic as long as the other members of the team don't have to pay a price for someone's individual brilliance.

In the mid 1980s, like every
other New South Welshman who
followed the game of Rugby
League, I would look forward to
the State of Origin, a series
where the best of the
Queenslanders took on the best
players from New South Wales. I
would look at the team on paper
and think that there was no way
that Queensland could beat
NSW. NSW was a team of
champions. The only problem
was the Queenslanders were a
champion team. The results
proved that.

Two heads are better than one

How it applies:

- Only when they are heading in the same direction.

- You can put together single items of anything to make multiples.

- But if those things don't have common ground and understanding.

- You have one thing 20 times.

- Not something that is a multiple of 20 strong.

During my time at the Australian Institute of Sport, I came into contact with an ex Airforce fighter pilot at one of our orientation camps. I asked him if he would talk to the group about performance anxiety - what it was like to stand on a runway waiting to be given the GO signal and trying to work out what that flight may bring. We spent from 7 pm until 3 am listening to his stories of commitment, bravery and teamwork. This is the story that I remember most vividly.

One of the skills a fighter pilot needs is the ability to read the information on the dashboard and, if needs be, transfer that information into actions. All this has to be done within a split second.

For every fighter pilot, there is also a navigator who sits in a control tower some miles away. The navigator can also see a set of gauges so he can give feedback to the pilot. This fighter pilot and his navigator had, over time, developed a strong trust in each other's ability.

One night, during a training flight, the pilot completed a particular manoeuvre, read the gauges and realised that they indicated that he was upside down and about to crash.

When, during the flight, the navigator realised the pilot thought himself in trouble, the navigator checked his gauges and immediately reassured the pilot that he was not, in fact, upside down and that all was well.

The pilot had to make a split second decision - to go with what he saw on his gauges and believed to be true, or to take his navigator's advice. He put his trust in his navigator.

The pilot said that he owes his life to his navigator. It was true teamwork that saved him that night.